Golden Hamsters

D1406578

BARRON'S

AUTHOR: PETER FRITZSCHE | PHOTOGRAPHER: REGINA KUHN

Contents

50 Always on the Move

Extras

Typical Golden Hamsters

With their button eyes, snub noses, and soft fur, Golden Hamsters look very cute. They are not cuddly pets, though, and are really not suitable playmates for young children. Nevertheless, they are interesting and cheerful little creatures who will quickly find their way into your heart.

It Has to Be a Golden Hamster

Thanks to their droll appearance and comical ways, Golden Hamsters are among the best-known and most popular pets today. The number of Golden Hamsters living in captivity is estimated to be ten million worldwide. In their native Syria people shake their heads in amused disbelief when they hear that Golden Hamsters are kept as children's pets in homes throughout Europe and North America. It was not so long ago that the little rodents first captured our hearts. And it all started out in a very small way.

A Golden Hamster for My Child?

If you are consulting this book, you may be toying with the idea of getting a Golden Hamster as a pet for your child. Before you head off to the nearest pet store you should think carefully about whether a hamster is really the right pet for your family, and in particular for your child. Based on my experience, Golden Hamsters are not suitable for children under 12 years of age. They might look cute and cuddly, but they really don't like to be handled. That's difficult for younger children to accept. In addition, Golden Hamsters are active at dusk and dawn (crepuscular) and at night (nocturnal); they want to sleep during the day.

The Golden Hamster is an ideal animal to watch. Naturally, you can also get close to her if you're careful, and gradually she will begin to overcome her initial shyness. That requires patience, something that younger children usually can't manage. However, if you are aware of these quirks, you will find the Golden Hamster to be an interesting pet that will bring your family a great deal of pleasure and enrich your life.

The Triumph of the Golden Hamster

It all began in the year 1930. At the Hebrew University of Jerusalem in Israel, researchers were trying to find a cure for leishmaniasis, a tropical disease also known as oriental sore. They needed Chinese Hamsters for their research but had difficulty breeding this dwarf species. Zoologist Israel Aharoni knew that dwarf hamsters were also found in neighboring Syria (although they were a different species). In April, an expedition set out to find the hamsters so that scientists could start breeding them in Jerusalem. Near the Syrian city of Aleppo, a sheikh offered his assistance and summoned workers, who started to dig in the surrounding wheat fields. After moving a lot of soil without success, they suddenly hit the jackpot. A nest with a mother hamster and 11 little pups was unearthed. The mother didn't look at all like a dwarf hamster, though. They called in a zoologist, who identified her as a Golden Hamster, a species he had known only from descriptions and pictures until then. This species was first mentioned in 1797 in a book by the physician Patrick Russell. Subsequently more than 40 years had passed before George Robert Waterhouse, an English zoologist in London, wrote the first scientific description of the Golden Hamster in 1839.

Golden Hamster: What's in a Name?

The scientific name of every animal or plant always consists of the genus name, which is capitalized, and the species name, which is written in lowercase. Waterhouse named the hamster *Mesocricetus auratus*, which means "golden medium hamster." To be scientifically precise, the name of the first person to describe the species and the year of its discovery are always included as well. Thus the full name of the Golden Hamster is *Mesocricetus auratus* Waterhouse 1839. This species is also called the Syrian Hamster.

This wild Golden Hamster cautiously leaves its burrow in the morning to search for food.

The First Successful Breeding

Until Golden Hamsters were rediscovered by Israeli researchers, no scientist had seen them alive. That's why Professor Aharoni was especially careful when placing the mother and her pups in a box. She was so stressed that she killed one of the pups right away. As a result, the mother was separated from her young. Mrs. Aharoni was able to feed the pups and keep them alive, but unfortunately a few more of them later escaped and drowned in a swimming pool in Jerusalem. That left three males and one female. The males were mated repeatedly with the female, and the breeding attempt was a success. The first seven young were born in captivity. They grew quickly and likewise were mated. After just one year there were 150 animals! All Golden Hamsters kept as pets today are descended from these brother-sister matings. As early as 1931 Golden Hamsters were brought from Jerusalem to France and England, and in 1938 Golden Hamsters took the United States by storm. Ten years later, in 1948, the first animals arrived in Germany, where there were immediately warnings about naturalizing a new species. It soon became clear that the animals couldn't survive Germany's cold, damp winters on their own.

Field Research at Halle

Until recently, the only Golden Hamsters kept in laboratories anywhere in the world were descendants of the original family from Jerusalem. There were two later expeditions to Syria that brought back animals as well, but they were not used for breeding. No one knew much about how Golden Hamsters lived in the wild. Then in 1999, Professor Rolf Gattermann, along with colleagues and students from the University of Halle in

With her cheek pouches full of lentils, this mother Golden Hamster hurries back along the shortest route to her pups in the burrow.

Germany, traveled to Syria in order to find the animals again. I was one of the members of this expedition. With the help of Syrian farmers, we searched there for Golden Hamsters, yet excavations in several wheat fields met with no success. Finally, we found a hamster in a lentil field at a depth of 24 inches (60 cm). It was a Golden Hamster, like those we had seen previously only in cages. We were overjoyed. We continued to dig in lentil fields and managed to trap a total of 19 wild Golden Hamsters, which we took back with us to Halle. There the animals reproduce just as well as their laboratory cousins. At present, we scientists are especially interested in comparing laboratory Golden Hamsters with the wild-living animals and studying their differences and similarities.

Golden Hamsters in the Wild

Wild-living Golden Hamsters can be found only in northern Syria and southern Turkey. They used to live exclusively in the steppes, but today the little rodents have invaded farmers' fields, where they have an easy time finding food. The local farmers aren't happy about that, so unfortunately they hunt the animals and even use chemical means to control them. Golden Hamsters prefer to live in lentil fields, but they can also be found in fields of wheat or sugar peas.

Confirmed Bachelors

The most important finding to emerge from observations of wild Golden Hamsters is that they are confirmed bachelors. Each one, whether male or female, lives in the burrow that it excavated. They have no interest in visiting each other, except when male and female come together briefly to mate. If two animals happen to meet, they get out of each other's way or there's trouble.

These pups, about three weeks old, are leaving their burrow in a wheat field for the first time. The plastic ring around the opening of the burrow lets the researcher record the activities of the animals without disturbing them.

The females live together with their young in the burrow until the babies are about four weeks old. Then the mother leaves the burrow to her offspring and digs herself a new one.

The Hamster in Its Burrow

The burrows are up to 3 feet (1 m) deep and have a vertical entrance, the so-called gravity pipe. There are several "rooms" in the burrow: a nesting chamber, a storage chamber, and a latrine. The nesting chamber is lined with dried plants. In the spring, Golden Hamsters leave their burrows to forage for food two to three hours before sunset. Females return to their burrows at night, whereas the males spend almost the entire night searching for a mate. The males check the burrows of several females, often traveling great distances. When the sun rises in the morning, the females emerge from their burrows for about an hour. Then they spend the day sleeping in their nest chamber until late afternoon.

Why Do Hamsters Hoard?

From June onward, it gets very dry in Syria, and the sun beats down mercilessly. The little rodents seldom leave their burrow then. Apparently they live off the food gathered in the spring. Until now, though, no one knew exactly how they survived this period. In winter when the temperature falls below 46°F (8°C), they hibernate: Then the Golden Hamster's body temperature, which is normally 98.6°F (37°C), drops to a few degrees above 32°F (0°C); this way the hamster conserves energy. Because of these extreme variations in climate, hamsters must hoard in order to survive seasons when food is scarce. Every four or five days they wake up to eat. *Hamster*, by the way, comes from the German word *hamstern*, which means "to hoard."

Golden Hamsters – Nocturnal Creatures

TIPS FROM
HAMSTER EXPERT
Peter Fritzsche

PAY ATTENTION TO ACTIVITY PERIODS
Golden Hamsters become active in the late afternoon or evening. Being disturbed during the day while they are asleep causes the animals real stress. Make sure you postpone cage cleaning, out-of-cage activity, and interaction of any type with the animals until late afternoon, after about 5 P.M.

TURNING NIGHT INTO DAY? The alternation of day and night is responsible for biorhythm in animals. It is possible to reverse this rhythm in Golden Hamsters. Scientists refer to this as inversion. To do this, only artificial light is used in the room where the cage is located; during the day, the room is kept dark (except for a red light), and at night the light is switched on. Within about ten days the animals get used to the new rhythm. The nocturnal-animal houses in many zoos make use of this technique. It is the only way to reverse the Golden Hamster's rhythm. Don't try it at home; making pet hamsters readjust like this is neither practical nor recommended.

Golden Hamsters as Pets

Even after decades of breeding, Golden Hamsters still display the characteristics and behavioral patterns that they share with their wild relatives.

Golden Hamsters are Unusual

When caring for Golden Hamsters, you should keep in mind some of their peculiarities.

Hamsters together: The Golden Hamster is a typical loner, whether living in the wild or in a cage.

Males and females come together briefly only to mate. Immediately after mating, the female chases the male away again. For this reason, Golden Hamsters must always be housed one to a cage.

Touch-me-nots: Golden Hamsters don't especially like being held. At our Institute we measured the heart rate of Golden Hamsters after other hamsters had been placed in their cage or they had been picked up and held. In both cases the number of heartbeats per minute rose dramatically. It took up to half an hour before the animals calmed down again. This is why you need a great deal of patience and sensitivity to get the hamster used to people.

Behavior: Because of their solitary lifestyle, Golden Hamsters don't display as wide a range of behaviors as animals that live in groups do. I explain the most important types of behavior in the Behavior Interpreter (see inside front cover).

Foraging: When Golden Hamsters leave the burrow, they look around cautiously in all directions for any signs of danger. Especially when they have to cross open country, they creep forward with their body pressed close to the ground. Once they reach shelter of vegetation, they run off quickly. Outside the burrow, Golden Hamsters can't risk taking the time to eat. They cram food into their cheek pouches and carry it back to the burrow.

There are now more than 40 varieties of Golden Hamster. Here is a Dark Eared White hamster with sooty ears.

Tip: In the wild, Golden Hamsters travel on the ground; they do not climb. Nevertheless, hamsters have an inborn "cliff avoidance behavior." When they come to a precipice like the edge of a table, they don't just keep going and fall off. Please don't test this at home with your Golden Hamster, though—it might end in disaster!

How Golden Hamsters Live

In the wild, Golden Hamsters are born in April or May, overwinter, and then mate the following year. Unfortunately, they don't live longer than one or two years. There are too many dangers, and the climate is too harsh. Golden Hamsters kept as pets can, with good care, live for three years and perhaps a bit more. That means you really can't bond with a Golden Hamster for long. Sad to say, no sooner have you grown to love your pet than it is already old.

How Did the Varieties of Golden Hamster Originate?

There are now more than 40 varieties or breeds of Golden Hamster (see pages 14–15). As a rule, only the wild type occurs naturally, having proved its evolutionary fitness over time. The different varieties that we know today arose through selective breeding. It's actually quite rare for individual animals to exhibit unusual traits spontaneously, such as a different color or longer hair. The breeder selects hamsters with these special traits, which are lost again in the wild, and propagates them. This way unusual coat colors or hair lengths are selectively bred.

Is a Golden Hamster **the Right Pet** for Me?

› I am at least 12 years old and am prepared to care for my hamster every day.	› I can occasionally let the hamster have out-of-cage time in our home.
› My parents will help me care for my Golden Hamster.	› I know that Golden Hamsters have a short life span of only about two years.
› I know that a Golden Hamster is not a playmate or a cuddly pet.	› My Golden Hamster will be the sole occupant of his or her cage; I will not put in a second hamster.
› I will accept the fact that my Golden Hamster doesn't like to be picked up.	› I will give my hamster a varied diet of seeds and grains, fruit, vegetables, and protein-rich food.
› I enjoy observing the natural behavior of animals.	› Every four weeks I will clean the hamster cage and all accessories thoroughly.
› We have enough room in our house for a large Golden Hamster cage.	› I know a small-animal veterinarian and will go there if my hamster gets sick.
› I will provide a stimulating cage environment for my Golden Hamster.	› I know someone who can take care of my hamster when I'm away.

Golden Hamster Characteristics

Adult Golden Hamsters grow to be about 7 inches (18 cm) long and weigh about 6 ounces (180 g). Females often weigh more than the males, which is somewhat unusual among mammals.

Anatomy of the Golden Hamster

External characteristics: The short tail is typical of almost all hamsters. In Golden Hamsters it reaches a maximum length of 0.4 inch (1 cm). The hamster's cheek pouches are another unique feature. These are outpocketings of the lining of the mouth that extend almost to the hind legs. When they are stuffed full, the Golden Hamster can carry almost an ounce (20 g) of grain in them. Back in the burrow, the hamster uses its front paws to push out the contents of the cheek pouches. Golden Hamsters have five toes on each foot. However, one toe on each front foot is rudimentary, so that there appear to be only four. The Golden Hamster's large incisors are a striking feature. These chisel-like teeth are considerably longer in the lower jaw than in the upper jaw. They grow continuously, so the hamster must have plenty of opportunity to keep them worn down.

Skeleton: The Golden Hamster's skeleton is rather delicate and fragile, so be careful not to let the animal fall from a height. Although hamsters exhibit cliff avoidance behavior, they sometimes jump down if they feel trapped. That can be disastrous, because they can't cushion their fall and thus can suffer broken bones.

Internal anatomy: There is nothing unusual about the structure of the internal organs of Golden Hamsters; anatomically they are similar to those of most mammals. In Golden Hamsters, the stomach is divided into a forestomach, where food is partially broken down, and a glandular stomach, where digestion occurs. Females have a two-part ("bicornuate") uterus, typical for rodents; young can develop in both parts.

Although Golden Hamsters have adorable shoe-button eyes, they can't see well with them. Hamsters are nearsighted and color-blind.

1 TEETH There's no mistaking the fact that Golden Hamsters are rodents. Give your pet plenty of opportunity to use those teeth and keep them worn down.

2 PAWS The little pads on the Golden Hamster's front and back feet cushion her weight when she walks. One toe on each forefoot is rudimentary.

3 CHEEK POUCHES This way the hamster always has a shopping bag handy. The pouches hold more than one-tenth of the hamster's body weight.

The Golden Hamster's Senses

Smell: The nose is the hamsters' most sensitive sensory organ. They can use it to distinguish smells much better than we humans. With the information obtained from smell, Golden Hamsters can recognize the presence of other hamsters, their sex, and their readiness to mate. In addition to olfactory cells in the nose, the animals have a special sensory organ in the head, the vomeronasal organ, which can even help them tell if they are related to another hamster. Golden Hamsters place scent marks around their burrow using feces, urine, and special glands. They have a so-called flank gland on either side of the body. If you carefully blow the fur aside, you can easily discern these dark-colored glands. Males in particular use them to mark their territory.

Hearing: Golden Hamsters have very acute hearing. They rely on it to sense impending danger when they emerge from their burrows. In addition to the sounds that we humans hear, Golden Hamsters, like bats, can detect ultrasonic frequencies. Young Golden Hamsters use high-pitched calls to signal their mother when they feel abandoned. Predators cannot hear these sounds.

Vision: Although Golden Hamsters have relatively large eyes, they cannot see very well. Because of their way of life, that's really not a problem. Although scientists still have some unanswered questions here, it seems that Golden Hamsters cannot see colors. Training experiments have shown that, at most, they are able to distinguish colors by differences in intensity. They recognize shades of green and yellow best. In addition, Golden Hamsters are nearsighted. They can only make out objects up to about 3 feet (1 m) away.

Touch: Naturally, Golden Hamsters also have sensory cells in the skin, with which they can register touch. Golden Hamsters are quite sensitive to pain, too. More interesting and important for them, however, are the tactile hairs on the muzzle. Golden Hamsters have five rows of these whiskers, called vibrissae. When the hamster is running, avoiding obstacles, or locating the entrance to the burrow, these are very important.

Golden Hamsters in Portrait

In addition to the wild-colored Golden Hamster, there are other varieties with different coat colors and patterns. If you've had no experience with hamsters, I recommend the wild type, which is easy to care for.

WILD-COLORED (AGOUTI) GOLDEN HAMSTER This variety is hard to tell from the wild relatives and is certainly the easiest to keep.

PANDA BEAR Because of the white band around the belly, this is also called the Banded Hamster. The white rings around the black eyes are especially attractive. Patterned hamsters like this one require more care than their wild-colored relatives.

SATIN This beautiful breed owes its name to the silky coat. There are several color varieties, most of them solid-colored. These hamsters are generally regarded as good-natured and get used to people easily.

PATTERNED These brown- or black-and-white (Dominant Spot) or tricolor (Calico) patterned hamsters are considered to be somewhat nippy and have a hard time adjusting to people.

TEDDY BEAR The Teddy Bear, or long-haired, hamster also comes in solid-colored varieties. Teddy Bear personalities range from good-natured to a bit lethargic.

DARK EARED WHITE These animals get their name from their ears, which appear to be covered with soot; apart from that, they are white. They are easy to care for and peaceable.

SELF This young solid-colored hamster is completely black. Selective breeding of unusual varieties like this one is no easy matter, and usually only experienced breeders manage it successfully.

ALBINO The white coat and red eyes are characteristics of this variety. Since they have a hard time camouflaging themselves, albinos are at a disadvantage in the wild, which is why they are so rarely found there.

Welcome Home

Before you bring your new companion home, a few preparations are in order. Hold a family meeting to decide where to put the Golden Hamster's cage. You'll learn everything you need to know about proper hamster husbandry in this chapter.

The Right Location for the Cage

Give careful thought to choosing a permanent location for the cage. As you already know (see page 9), Golden Hamsters are active at dusk and dawn (crepuscular) or at night (nocturnal) and like to sleep during the day. This means you should find a reasonably quiet spot. The best place is a room that is not used much during the day and doesn't get a lot of traffic, so living rooms or children's rooms aren't really suitable. Of course, this makes the search difficult if not impossible. For one thing, your children naturally want their pet nearby. Then, too, conditions in your home usually limit your options, so the cage often winds up in the children's room anyway.

At least try to choose a quiet corner there. Avoid exposing the cage to loud noise from a television or stereo. If possible, the cage shouldn't be near a window, either. Golden Hamsters don't like harsh light or direct sun. In addition to being too bright, it could make the cage overheat in the summer months. The temperature in the cage should not exceed 77°F (25°C). If that proves difficult in the summer, you can cool the cage by draping damp towels over it. Low temperatures, on the other hand, are not a problem. This means you needn't worry about putting the cage in an unheated room, even in winter. To make sure the hamster remains active, though, don't let the temperature drop below about 59°F (15°C) for any length of time.

It's best to place the cage at eye level so that you can observe your Golden Hamster easily. Ideally, move the hamster cage against a wall and darken another side; your hamster will appreciate it.

The Golden Hamster's Home

After the question of location has been resolved, you can start looking for a suitable cage. My recommendations will help you here.

Tips for Buying a Cage

When choosing a home for your hamster, the first rule is that the cage can be too small, but never too large.

Cage size: In general, the cage should offer a minimum of about 3 square feet (3,000 cm^2) of floor space. That means at least 32 inches (80 cm) wide and 16 inches (40 cm) deep. Smaller cages are often sold as "hamster cages." Bear in mind

that these are suitable for dwarf hamsters at best. The cage should be at least 16 inches (40 cm) high. After all, you have to find room for the nest box, climbing equipment, an exercise wheel, and perhaps additional upper levels.

Combining cages: One larger cage can also be replaced by two smaller ones. If you have enough room for it, this option is preferable. The two cages are then connected by a plastic tube so that your pet can easily move between the two areas. This is also more like a natural hamster burrow. The sleeping nest is in one cage and the food storage area is in the other.

Connecting cages the right way: The connecting tunnel should not be more than 12 inches (30 cm) long in order for you to clean it easily. With longer connecting tunnels, ventilation becomes a problem. However, there are flexible plastic tubes that even have small holes for ventilation. Ask for perforated drainage pipe at the home improvement center; it's just right for your purposes. You can also use PVC piping (from the home improvement center) 2 inches (5 cm) in diameter as connecting tunnels. Your Golden Hamster will love these tubes, because they are very much like the connecting tunnels of a hamster burrow.

Multilevel cages: Tubes can also connect several levels in a large cage. To do this, install wooden or, better yet, plastic shelves in the cage.

A cage with built-in shelves offers the Golden Hamster more floor space. An assortment of toys and accessories keep him fit.

Two cages can be easily joined by a tube. This way the Golden Hamster can have a home with several rooms, just like the earthen burrows in the wild.

Tube systems are always a hit with Golden Hamsters. Give your little friends a treat like this; it keeps them healthy and fit.

The distance between shelves should be at least 8 inches (20 cm). Pet stores carry multilevel cages. Upper levels made of wire mesh or bars are not good for little hamster paws. Alternatively, you can connect the floors with small ladders.

An Aquarium as a Golden Hamster Home?

A converted aquarium can be used to keep a hamster, provided it is large enough, but the disadvantages outweigh the advantages. On the plus side, most of the bedding stays in the cage when the hamster digs and burrows. In addition, the occupant is protected from drafts and noise and can't scale the side walls, get hurt, or escape. If the tank is at least 12 inches (30 cm) high, it does not need a cover. However, you can't put anything (like the nest box) against the wall that the hamster could climb on. And the disadvantages? First of all, ventilation in the tank is poor because air cannot circulate. The larger the tank, the better the

ventilation. For a Golden Hamster, you need an aquarium at least 40 inches (1 m) long. Cleaning is also difficult: You have to remove everything and wash out the entire tank. If you keep your hamster in an aquarium, watch for any unusual behavior and be prepared to take remedial action right away (see page 49).

If You're Handy, **Build the Cage Yourself**

Start with a bottom tray that you have purchased or made yourself by gluing together sheets of acrylic plastic. Cut the floor, rear wall, and sides from boards 1/2 to 3/4 inch (15–20 mm) thick. Then for the front, fit an acrylic sheet into grooves cut in the sides. Cover the frame of the lid with wire screen and fasten it to the rear wall with hinges.

Equipment and Accessories

To make sure your Golden Hamster feels right at home, you have to set up the cage properly. When it comes to the basic necessities, the pet store has a wide assortment on hand for you.

1 Hamster Nest Box

Because Golden Hamsters are used to living in dark burrows in the wild, they definitely need a hiding place. A cage without a nest box puts the animals under constant stress. I recommend a wooden nest box. Plastic or ceramic nest boxes are not advisable because moisture builds up in them, and that's not good for the hamster's health. Pet stores carry various types of wooden nest boxes. The box needs only one entrance, and the hamster can do without a window. The floor area should measure approximately 8 × 4 inches (20 × 10 cm), and the box should be about 4 inches (10 cm) high. A flat roof is ideal; then your hamster can climb up on it easily. To keep the nest box from sliding around in the cage constantly, simply place a rock on the roof.

2 Eating Area

Although in their natural habitat hamsters forage everywhere for food, a food bowl makes it easier for you to keep track of how much you feed. A porcelain or ceramic bowl is best because it is fairly sturdy. The bowl should be at least 2 inches (5–6 cm) in diameter and $\frac{3}{4}$ inch (2 cm) deep. A lip that curves slightly inward prevents the food from falling out.

3 Water Bottle

The hamster should always have fresh water available in the cage. Don't put it in a bowl, though; instead, use a standard water bottle. The bottle can be attached conveniently to the outside of the cage. This way the hamster can't chew on it, and it can be filled more easily. Select a bottle with a double ball-point vacuum valve.

4 Bedding

In my experience, small-animal bedding from the pet store is best. Sawdust, garden peat, cat litter, and similar products are not recommended. Along with the bedding, there should always be a bundle of hay in one corner of the cage. The Golden Hamster will be glad to carry it off to line the nest box. Avoid the synthetic fiber bedding sold as "hamster fluff." Its fine threads can entangle an animal or even wrap around a leg and cut off circulation.

5 Hamster Toilet

Pet stores sell corner litter pans made of ceramic. They are filled with sand, which can be changed easily. Naturally, you can try to train your hamster to use it, and some actually do accept the toilet easily. Don't be disappointed, though, if your pet has other ideas. He may seek out a toilet area on his own, or he may just scatter his droppings around the cage. Although wild hamsters usually have a latrine area in their burrow, they may behave quite differently in a cage.

What to Look For When Buying a Hamster

At last! The cage is ready and its occupant can move in. If you keep a few basics in mind when buying your hamster and bringing him home, you and your pet will be off to a good start.

Pet Store or Breeder?

The first place most buyers look is the nearest pet store or a general retail store with a pet department. The sales staff is usually well trained and should be able to answer all your questions. The animals offered for sale come mainly from professional breeders or sometimes from hobbyists. You can also buy your hamster directly from a breeder. Animal shelters often have older Golden Hamsters awaiting new homes. Shelters are happy to place their animals in good hands.

What Must I Be Aware of When Buying a Hamster?

Try to visit several pet stores and compare them. Are the animals being cared for properly? Is the lighting subdued enough? Do the animals have a nest box where they can hide? Do they have enough food and fresh water? The right time of day is also important when buying a hamster. Golden Hamsters don't become active until late in the day, so postpone your visit until late afternoon. Take your time observing the animals; spend at least 15–20 minutes with them. Pick out your favorite and make sure he or she meets the requirements for a healthy hamster (see Checklist in the box opposite).

It's so Hard to Decide

Aside from appearance, the various Golden Hamster breeds (see pages 14–15) differ only slightly in behavior. Choosing a hamster is thus a matter of personal taste. I always recommend the wild-type Golden Hamster for children and novice hamster keepers. This variety is easy to care for and usually less susceptible to disease. It's best to pick a young Golden Hamster.

By four weeks of age, little hamsters are independent and are weaned from their mothers. An animal that is four to eight weeks old, then,

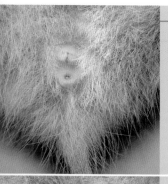

1 The easiest way to tell the difference between the sexes is by the distance from the anus to the genital opening. In females this distance is smaller.

2 In males the distance between the anus and the penis is larger. In summer, you can recognize the male by his prominent testicles.

would be ideal. If the dealer can't tell you their exact age, your only recourse is to compare them with fully grown animals. Golden Hamsters weigh about 2 ounces (55 g) at five weeks of age, at which time they are about half as large as adults.

Male or Female?

When it comes to caring for the animals, there is very little difference between males and females. Females have a slight odor when they are in heat. Sex is often difficult to determine in hamsters. During the warm months, the testicles of the males protrude a bit and can be seen from above. In males the distance between the genital and anal openings is greater than in females.

Bringing Your Hamster Home

Buy a travel carrier for small animals so you can transport your hamster safely and with as little stress as possible. The hamster can easily escape from the cardboard box provided by the dealer. This carrier will come in handy at home as temporary housing when you're cleaning the cage or going to the veterinarian. Ask the dealer to give you a bit of old bedding from the display cage to put in the carrier. The familiar scent will calm the animal. For a long trip, a slice of apple or a piece of carrot is important as a source of moisture. A water bottle is not recommended because it can leak. The carrier must not overheat in the summer, so an air-conditioned car would be ideal. Put the hamster on the backseat of the car, not in the trunk.

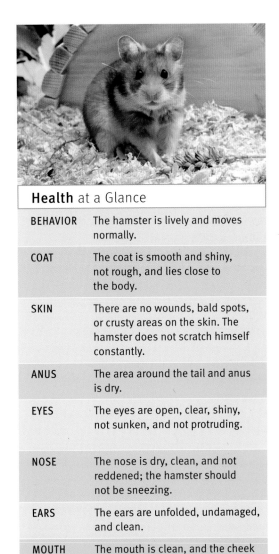

Health at a Glance

BEHAVIOR	The hamster is lively and moves normally.
COAT	The coat is smooth and shiny, not rough, and lies close to the body.
SKIN	There are no wounds, bald spots, or crusty areas on the skin. The hamster does not scratch himself constantly.
ANUS	The area around the tail and anus is dry.
EYES	The eyes are open, clear, shiny, not sunken, and not protruding.
NOSE	The nose is dry, clean, and not reddened; the hamster should not be sneezing.
EARS	The ears are unfolded, undamaged, and clean.
MOUTH	The mouth is clean, and the cheek pouches are empty. If the pouches are full, wait until the hamster has emptied them.

Acclimation Made Easy

You've brought your little Golden Hamster home safe and sound. Now to win his trust, it's important that you proceed slowly and carefully.

Moving in to a New Home

Once you've arrived home, gently place the hamster in his new home right away. Put the old bedding from the travel carrier into the cage. If the hamster is in a cardboard box from the dealer, put this in the cage and open it carefully. That way he can creep out on his own.

Do not disturb: After the enormous stress of the move, your new companion needs a lot of rest! And you have to make sure he gets it. Even if you find it difficult, disturb him as little as possible for at least a week. Sit down very quietly in front of the cage, and avoid any sudden movements or high-pitched noises.

Approach with care: Don't fiddle with anything in or on the cage. Except for providing food and water, change nothing during the first few days. Don't put the food in the cage until the hamster is in his nest box. On no account should you pick him up. He's sure to have hidden in his nest box immediately after being put in his cage. Gradually he'll emerge and begin marking his new territory with his scent. Let him investigate the contents of his cage at his own pace. Forgo any out-of-cage time during these first weeks. If the hamster stops scurrying nervously around the cage after a few days, rests in his nest box during the day, and begins his activities with stretching and yawning, then he has adjusted to his new home.

The Right Way to Make Friends

Once your hamster is familiar with his cage, it's time for him to get used to his caregiver. The hamster should realize that he has nothing to fear from you or your hand. For this to happen, you really do have to proceed very slowly and with a great deal of patience.

First step: Always move slowly and quietly so that you don't upset the hamster with sudden movements. Leave the cage door closed at first. Try to offer him a particularly tasty treat through the cage bars, such as a piece of apple or carrot, a peanut, or—very effective—a mealworm. A dab of cottage cheese on your index finger is also tempting for a Golden Hamster. Now the hamster has to decide between retreating and approaching. He may suddenly begin to groom himself. Biologists call this "displacement behavior." If an animal is unable to choose between two opposing behaviors, it vents the pent-up energy in a completely different behavior. Soon, however, curiosity and the food will win out, and he'll take the morsel from your finger.

Building trust: The initial hurdles have been overcome. Now you can take the next step and open the cage door. If the hamster runs into his nest box, don't pick it up and force him out. Rub your hand with bedding from the cage to give it a familiar scent. Then quietly place your hand in the cage and wait until the hamster approaches and sniffs at it.

TAKE YOUR TIME You can win the Golden Hamster's trust only with lots of patience and a cautious approach. Don't disturb him at all in the first few weeks, regardless of how curious you are. Be very careful when feeding him and checking the cage for leftover fresh foods, and don't do this when the hamster is asleep. Then you can watch him in the evening through the cage bars. Speak to your new companion in a soft, calm voice.

TEMPT HIM WITH TREATS For the second phase of acclimation, remember that "the way to a hamster's heart is through his stomach." Use a wooden toothpick to pass fresh greens, pieces of fruit, or a mealworm through the cage bars to your Golden Hamster. If he nibbles at the treat, the next time you can try passing it through the opened cage door. Then give him the treat without a toothpick, using your thumb and index finger.

GETTING USED TO YOUR HAND Let your little friend sniff your hand to his heart's content, even without food. This works best if you rub your hands beforehand with a bit of bedding from the cage.

Good Manners

The first weeks with your Golden Hamster are now behind you; with a lot of patience, you have managed to get your pet to approach you, even if warily, and respond to you less timidly than in the beginning.

My Friend, the Golden Hamster

On page 24, I described how you should go about making friends with your Golden Hamster. At some point your hamster will have overcome his shyness and climbed onto your hand. When, after a few "sittings," he is completely used to your hand, you can stroke his neck and back carefully with one finger. If he likes it, then you have won his friendship. The time it takes to achieve this successful result can vary.

Differences among breeds: Golden Hamsters are little individuals, too, and each one has his or her own personality and mannerisms. Some

acclimate easily, whereas others take longer to overcome their shyness. The patterned breeds are said to have a harder time adjusting to people. That's why I recommend that novice hamster keepers start with a wild-colored Golden Hamster.

Avoid too many caregivers: During the acclimation period, it doesn't do your Golden Hamster any good if different people keep trying to befriend him. Younger children in particular are sometimes a bit too lively, which might frighten your new companion.

Picking up and Carrying

Actually, you should never have to pick up or carry an unwilling hamster in your hands. Whenever possible, the hamster should do everything voluntarily, even climbing into your hand without coercion. At our Institute, experiments with heart rate measurements have shown that grasping and picking up the hamster, which scientists refer to as handling, is very stressful for the animal. Yet here, too, it helps to be gentle and use the correct technique, because it's not always possible to avoid picking up the hamster.

The tumbler trick: Your Golden Hamster will have to be moved when you clean the cage, if not sooner. This is easier with the help of a container.

You could use a tumbler, a cup, or a box large enough to hold the hamster. Rub this container with a bit of bedding from the cage. Then hold

Cupping the Golden Hamster securely in your hands when carrying him around reduces his stress.

in front of the hamster and bring your other hand up behind him. The animal will try to get away and, searching for an escape route, will climb into the container. Now put your hand over the container and you can transport the hamster.

Picking up properly: As soon as the hamster is used to your hand—for instance if he sniffs it readily or even climbs on it and lets you pet him—you can carry him in your bare hands without worry. Don't use gloves. You can't get the proper feel for a hamster's sensitive little body with them. As a result, you risk not holding him tightly enough and dropping him, or you could hurt him by gripping him too tightly. Grasp the hamster from behind and above with both bare hands, thus forming a sort of protective cave around him. Then bring your hands together under the hamster and lift him out of the cage. You always have to be careful when doing this that he doesn't jump out of your hands. If the cage is too small or if you have to get the hamster out of a tight spot, you can also grasp him from behind with one hand, bringing your thumb and index finger together behind his front legs (see photos, page 40) and slide the other hand beneath him. Please don't use any other method to carry the animal. It's better not to grasp the hamster by the loose skin on the back of the neck ("scruffing"), as is sometimes recommended. This method takes practice and the expertise of a breeder or veterinarian.

Golden Hamsters and Other Pets

TIPS FROM
HAMSTER EXPERT
Peter Fritzsche

FOLLOW THE BASIC RULES Say good-bye to any ideas you have about housing cats and dogs with hamsters. Hamsters are and always will be loners and cannot be persuaded otherwise. Consequently, the most important precaution is to keep all animals, regardless of species, away from your Golden Hamster.

CATS It stands to reason that keeping cats and hamsters in the same household is difficult, because cats must be kept out of the room where the Golden Hamster's cage is located. It is part of a cat's instinctive behavior to view hamsters as prey. Even the mere presence of a cat is very stressful for the hamster and not advisable for any length of time.

DOGS Dogs are less of a problem if they show no interest in your hamster, but even they shouldn't be allowed near the Golden Hamster especially during out-of-cage time.

FISH AND OTHER FRIENDS Naturally, keeping other small animals in cages, terrariums, or aquariums usually presents no problem.

Golden Hamster Babies

It is certainly not my intention to give you any instructions on how to breed Golden Hamsters here. That task is best left to professional breeders. In some countries, the sale of the offspring is regulated, and furthermore these animals are routinely checked by veterinary inspectors. Perhaps, though, you've chosen a particularly large female, and not long after returning home, you hear squeaking coming from the hamster cage. A glance inside confirms your suspicions: You've got baby hamsters. But even if you haven't brought home a pregnant animal, it is always interesting for hamster lovers to learn how Golden Hamsters reproduce.

Mating

Like most mammals, Golden Hamster females are not always ready to mate. In the wild, the time for reproduction is restricted to a few months in the spring. When they are kept in a heated room with sufficient light, females as well as males are, in principle, capable of reproducing all year long. The females come into heat for several hours approximately every four days, usually from the evening until about the middle of the following day. After mating, the female no longer tolerates the male, and the breeder has to remove him. In the wild, the female chases the male away.

Pregnancy and Birth

With her brief gestation period (as pregnancy in animals is termed), the female Golden Hamster might hold a record among mammals. It lasts just 16 days. During this period, the expectant mother gathers nesting material and food for her future offspring. If you have a pregnant female, you should be sure to provide her with material for building a nest. She'll gladly accept soft absorbent paper (such as facial tissues). The pregnant hamster needs additional protein in her diet, but fresh foods should also be on the daily menu. Shortly before giving birth, the female becomes quieter and comes out of her nest box less often. At this point you shouldn't disturb the mother-to-be. Don't clean the cage, either! Birth usually takes place in the morning. As a rule, eight tiny, naked young (called pups) are born.

When they're in heat, Golden Hamster females are very patient, but only for as long as it takes to mate.

Raising the Young

At birth, a pup weighs no more than about 0.1 ounce (2.5 g). The newborns can barely move. They try to wriggle, headfirst, toward their mother's nipples. Then they hold on to the nipples with their tiny incisors. The mother leaves her litter only to eat. Please don't disturb the happy family. Naturally, you're dying to know what the babies look like and how many there are. It's best, though, to wait until the day after the birth, when the mother is outside, before taking a peek inside the nest box. As soon as the mother leaves the pups, they will call out for her. We humans can't hear these sounds because, like the calls of bats, they are in the ultrasonic range.

1 JUST BORN This newborn Golden Hamster, just one day old, is naked and pink. His eyes are still closed, the eyelids stuck shut. Hamsters are helpless at birth ("altricial") and cannot regulate their body temperature. Without their mother's warmth, they die. The mother is very sensitive to disturbances and can neglect her pups or even eat them.

2 ONE WEEK OLD At seven days of age, the young are already using their front and back legs to crawl short distances. Their eyes are still shut, but they can now hear and smell. They can lift their head and roll over when placed on their back. Gradually they try to nibble on bits of food. Their coat color is beginning to appear.

3 ALMOST FULLY GROWN By three weeks of age, a Golden Hamster is independent. All senses are functioning. The pups can feed themselves and are no longer nursed by their mother. Now the young leave the burrow for the first time. In the wild, the mother separates from her offspring a week later. As pets, they should get their own cage soon.

Young Hamster—Old Hamster

It is fascinating to observe how quickly Golden Hamsters develop at the beginning of their all-too-brief life.

Young Golden Hamsters

When the pups are just two days old, their coat begins to grow. At first, only a grayish fuzz is visible. It continues to grow and after about two weeks the coat has turned brown. On the second day the babies also start to move their front legs. By the time they are six days old, they can move their hind legs, too. At just two weeks of age, the young Golden

Hamsters are able to leave the nest by themselves. Their birth weight has doubled by the sixth day, and at 14 days they weigh about 0.5 ounce (15 g). The first sense to develop is their ability to smell. As tests have shown, they can recognize their own nest by its smell when they are just five days old. The ear flaps have also unfolded by then. Sight takes a bit longer to develop. The eyes don't start to open until 14 days after birth. The young are nursed by their mother for about three weeks. After that they eat only solid food. They begin to nibble on morsels of food when they are about 13 days old. The pups can sometimes be seen chewing on fecal pellets. There's nothing wrong with this; it's how they ingest minerals that are still contained in the feces. In the wild, after the young are fairly self-sufficient at three weeks of age, they begin to make short trips outside their burrow. With pet hamsters, the young are allowed to remain with their mother until they are four weeks old. After that they are weaned and get their own cage.

Adult Golden Hamsters

Females are sexually mature by the time they are about four weeks old; males take a bit longer, usually six weeks. After males and females are segregated, siblings of the same sex can still share a cage for a while. With time, however, quarreling

These young Golden Hamsters are about three weeks old. They still live together peacefully, but soon they will become quarrelsome and want to live alone.

and biting become more frequent. After about six weeks, the pups should be separated. At this age they can also be purchased in a pet store. It is possible to try to mate males and females once they have reached two months of age. Golden Hamsters don't live very long. In the wild, they are born during the period from March to May, survive just one winter, and die in the autumn of their second year. As pets, they are well cared for and live under ideal conditions—plenty of food, no enemies, and comfortable temperatures—so it's not unusual for Golden Hamsters in captivity to live for three or even four years.

Old Golden Hamsters

Don't be dismayed or saddened if your hamster begins showing signs of age when he is just two years old. How can you tell when the hamster is getting old? Of course, it helps if you know approximately when your pet was born. It's also easy to recognize signs of aging in behavior: The hamster no longer comes out of the nest box in the afternoon or evening as usual, but delays until much later. He moves more slowly and cautiously, and he uses his exercise wheel less often. Eating and hoarding are no longer so important. His appearance also changes: His coat becomes rough. He starts to lose hair, beginning on his head. He may develop flaky spots on his skin and may also lose weight. Be very considerate of your old friend now, don't disturb him, and give him his favorite foods.

A rough coat, weight loss, and decreased activity are signs of aging in hamsters. These "senior citizens" need lots of rest.

Saying Good-bye to **Your Golden Hamster**

WHEN GOLDEN HAMSTERS DIE If you always pay close attention to your pet, sooner or later you'll notice that he's beginning to age. If you are not certain, ask a veterinarian. Older hamsters often get diseases like tumors, too, and then it is better to put an end to their suffering. Try to explain gently to your children that death is a part of life. Let them know that Golden Hamsters don't live very long, and prepare them early on for the inevitable. Check your local laws to see if you can bury your pet in your yard, garden, or some other favorite spot. Other options include pet cemeteries and cremation.

The Golden Rules of Hamster Care

A healthy diet and plenty of exercise are prerequisites for a long life in Golden Hamsters. When caring for your pet, you have to find the right balance. Too much of a good thing can be just as harmful as too little. That's why optimal nutrition and proper care are so important.

What Do Golden Hamsters Eat in the Wild?

The best time for Golden Hamsters in the wild begins as winter ends, which means the weeks from the end of February to the beginning of March. After months of cold weather, the sun warms the soil, and the hamsters emerge from their burrows. By now they have used up their stores of food, and hunger drives them to the surface, where fresh food beckons.

The Hamster in the Field

Golden Hamsters used to live in the steppes, where they sometimes had to travel long distances to find food. Nowadays, however, farming is carried out wherever possible. If the Golden Hamster has its burrow in one of these cultivated fields, the food grows conveniently right next door. Golden Hamsters are particularly fond of lentil and chickpea fields, but their burrows are also found in wheat fields. Golden Hamsters leave the protection of the burrow only to forage for food or when they're on the lookout for a breeding partner. They seldom eat outside the burrow; instead, they carry their food home. Fresh plants of all kinds and cereal grains are their favorites. Golden Hamsters happily devour small insects and worms, too, to satisfy their protein requirement. By June the sun blazes mercilessly and dries up everything. Then Golden Hamsters find little except seeds. Fresh food is available only when fruits like melons are planted in the fields. In the burrow, the hoarded food is stored in a special chamber. The burrow is very tidy. After all, the food has to last through the entire fall and winter. This well-kept burrow is also the reason that Golden Hamsters rarely suffer from infections.

Good Nutrition

Food for pet Golden Hamsters is of three types. Dry food consisting of seeds and dried plants makes up about half of the major portion. The other half is composed primarily of fresh foods. A small but significant portion of the hamster's diet is protein of animal origin.

Dry Vegetable Foods

Pet stores sell a variety of dry food mixes for small animals or even specifically for Golden Hamsters. As a rule, you can feel confident buying this food and feeding it to your pet.

Homegrown Hamster Food

DELICATESSEN Spoil your pet with fresh plants collected from your yard. Plants like dandelion, clover, plantain (all types), daisy, mint, shepherd's purse, and parsley are ideal for feeding to your hamster. Don't gather plants from lawns frequented by dogs or collect them along heavily traveled roads.

GROW IT YOURSELF You can also raise some plants yourself. You don't have to have a garden to do this. Seeds of many broadleaf plants as well as wheat and grass seeds can be made to sprout in a bowl with a bit of absorbent paper or some soil. Keep it evenly moist, and the first green shoots will soon appear. A little plant fertilizer is helpful at this point. As soon as the plants are large enough, just place the bowl in your pet's cage.

Mixed-seed diets: This dry food consists mainly of various cereal grains, rolled oats, and sunflower seeds, as well as specially manufactured food flakes. Make sure that the food contains little or no sugar. Diseases of the gastrointestinal tract as well as diabetes can usually be traced back to excess sugar in the diet. The fat content of the food is also important and should not be too high. Sunflower seeds and nuts are known to contain a lot of fat. Good hamster food also contains a certain percentage of animal protein, often in the form of dried meat or dried insects. Don't buy food in bulk. Food that has been stored too long can get moldy or be infested by other small or large pests like meal moths. That's why you have to keep the food in airtight plastic containers.

Tip: You might like to compare the composition of different commercial hamster diets. To do this, you can set up a table in which you enter the percentages of nutrients in the individual mixes. These are printed on the package label. Then compare the following basic components: carbohydrate (major nutrient, about 65 percent), crude protein (protein content, 15–20 percent), crude fat (very little, up to 5 percent), crude fiber (roughage, 8–10 percent), and crude ash (minerals and trace elements, about 4 percent). The values given here in parentheses are suggested amounts.

Changing foods: Feel free to switch between different commercial hamster diets. When you do this, observe your pet. Does she have particular preferences? Keep in mind, though, that her favorite food is not always the most healthful.

Golden Hamsters don't just eat from a bowl. Your little friend can enjoy nibbling on a nice ear of wheat.

Creeping Inchplant (*Callisia repens*) is the name of this houseplant, native to Latin America. It is easy to propagate, and your hamster might find it tasty, too.

Don't mix the food yourself: It takes a lot of work, and getting the right composition is no easy matter.

How much to feed: It is difficult to say how much food is enough. That's why there should always be dry food in the bowl. An adult Golden Hamster eats about two to three teaspoons a day. If the food disappears quickly, don't forget that you are keeping a hamster—check the cage from time to time for hoarded food. In addition to commercial food, your Golden Hamster might also appreciate a little piece of dry bread. It's good for keeping her incisors in shape. The hamster also eats dry plants, which means hay. This provides her with the crude fiber necessary in her diet. It is ideal if the hay also contains meadow plants.

Nutritious Fresh Foods

Your Golden Hamster requires the vitamins and minerals contained in fresh foods. In the wild, the animals also satisfy their need for water with fresh foods. If you feed fruits and vegetables regularly,

your Golden Hamster won't touch her water bottle. In addition to carrots, apples, and cucumbers, you should offer berries and wild plants. Feed lettuce and chicory only on occasion. Fresh foods also include branches from fruit trees like apple, pear, or cherry that you can place in the cage, leaves and all. In addition to supplying nutrients and fiber, they provide your pet with a wonderful way to exercise her incisors. You can't stock the cage with fresh foods, but feeding them in small amounts in the evening is ideal for your hamster. Be sure to move the leftovers from the cage the following day! Unfortunately, mistakes made in feeding fresh foods frequently cause gastrointestinal ailments with diarrhea. That's why you need to be especially careful here.

Essential Dietary Protein

Even in the wild, Golden Hamsters are not strict vegetarians. Although animal protein is already found in most commercial hamster diets, Golden

Hamsters need additional amounts from time to time. One to three times a week, you should give your pet something like unsweetened cottage cheese, cream cheese, ground beef, or dog food. Place a little bit—as much as the hamster will eat right away—in a small container. As soon as she has finished eating, remove the container from the cage. You can also offer her a little portion on a toothpick or your finger. Naturally, that will also strengthen the bond between you and your hamster.

Live foods: You can see an entirely different side of your pet when you offer her live food. Best of all are larvae of the darkling beetle, called mealworms, which are available in pet stores.

They are sold by weight, so ask for 1.75 ounces (50 g) to start with. At home, put the mealworms in a plastic dish with a perforated lid. If you feed them rolled oats and hard bread, the larvae can be kept for weeks. Remove a larva with tweezers or with your fingers and feed it directly to your hamster. You shouldn't give your Golden Hamster more than three or four mealworms a week, because they are very high in fat. Other options are the larger larvae of *Zoophobas* beetles, also known as giant mealworms or superworms, as well as live crickets; you can buy them in pet stores, too.

Pampering with Snacks?

Of course you love your hamster and want to pamper her. How about something sweet, a piece of chocolate or one of the colorful snacks that are sold in pet stores? No, thanks! Restrain yourself, no matter how hard it is. These supposed rewards shorten the hamster's life. Don't even start down this path with young animals. Golden Hamsters can develop diabetes or other metabolic disorders. They enjoy natural treats, though, like small pieces of apple, a peanut, or occasionally a raisin.

Golden Hamsters don't just eat plants. They also enjoy mealworms. Don't feed these too often, though, or your pet will get fat.

Tasty Foods for Your Hamster

Although Golden Hamsters have a fairly strong stomach, certain foods are harmful while others are good for them. The most important rules for feeding are summarized below.

Good Choices

(+) Feed primarily dry vegetable foods like pea flakes, wheat grains, rolled oats, lentils, and corn as well as dry bread and crispbread. Also offer fresh hay and dried herbs.

(+) Fresh daily: cucumbers, carrots, zucchini, soy sprouts, beets, and fruit supply the necessary vitamins.

(+) Dandelion leaves, daisies, shepherd's purse, cat grass, and plantain are rich in minerals. Branches from fruit trees are good to chew on and promote strong teeth.

(+) Cottage cheese, natural yogurt, egg whites, and an occasional mealworm supply an adequate amount of animal protein.

Better Not

(−) Do not feed sweets like chocolate, gummy candies, or "yogurt drops"— they will make your hamster sick. Avoid sweet or spicy baked goods, salted nuts, acorns, and chestnuts.

(−) Feed sparingly: foods high in fat or calories such as egg yolk, nuts, pumpkin seeds, sunflower seeds, cheese, avocados, insect larvae, cooked or raw noodles, "hamster waffles," dog biscuits, dog food, and cat food.

(−) Avoid cabbage, carrot tops, tomato leaves, potatoes, spinach, and leeks.

(−) Do not feed fruits that are high in fruit acids, such as peaches, apricots, nectarines, pineapples, and all citrus fruits.

Golden Hamster Care Made Easy

Golden Hamsters are naturally clean animals that are meticulous about their grooming. As a pet owner, just a bit of effort on your part will help to keep your little friend looking her best.

The Well-Groomed Golden Hamster

Golden Hamsters in the wild are very rarely dirty or infested with parasites. Not only are they extremely careful about keeping their burrow clean, but they also groom themselves thoroughly and often. You can observe this in your pet especially after she wakes up. First she stretches and yawns contentedly; then she usually starts grooming her coat right away. The animals use their front as well as their back paws to do this, with the front paws being used one at a time or simultaneously. The hamster nibbles at her coat wherever she can reach with her mouth, licks it, or salivates on it. Young animals not yet able to manage this by themselves are licked clean by their mother.

The hamster grooms herself not only when she wakes up, but also after emptying her cheek pouches and always after eating.

How Hamsters Groom Themselves

The sequence of steps Golden Hamsters follow when grooming themselves is not accidental, but rather is genetically determined. You can verify this yourself with a little observational experiment. The five most common grooming activities are (1) licking, (2) nibbling, (3) simultaneous grooming with both forepaws, (4) grooming with one forepaw, and (5) scratching with the hind foot. First, watch your Golden Hamster as she grooms

herself and record the sequence of activities by number. Second, determine how often each grooming activity occurs. That will let you know precisely how your little friend likes to groom herself. Using a table, you can find out how often one activity follows another. For instance, how often does 1 follow 2, 1 follow 3, 1 follow 4, and so on. You will discover that these figures differ clearly and that hamsters prefer certain grooming sequences. Scientists have found that, in healthy hamsters with no behavioral problems, grooming activities 3 and 4 occur most often and the animals usually groom themselves in this sequence. Behavioral scientists call a study like this a "sequence diagram"; when correctly recorded, it can even be used to recognize behavior problems in a hamster.

Wellness for Golden Hamsters

The most important part of caring for a Golden Hamster is observing your pet carefully. This way you can be quick to spot any changes, for example

Weigh Your Golden Hamster Regularly

WEIGH ONCE A WEEK Regular weighing will give you important information about the health and well-being of your pet. A kitchen scale with digital display is best for this. Place the Golden Hamster in a container with high sides and subtract the weight of the container from the total result. Record the weight on a calendar.

PERFECTLY GROOMED Golden Hamsters love to groom themselves. That's why parasites that attack fur and skin have a hard time with them. The animals follow an instinctive program when grooming. They make use of all four paws and their teeth in the process, but they use their front paws the most, either simultaneously or one at a time. Sometimes it's hard to tell if they are cleaning their muzzle or licking their paws.

DEXTEROUS Our hamster looks cute scratching behind her ears with her hind paw. Golden Hamsters use their hind legs far less often than their front paws for grooming. No wonder: The range of motion of the hind limbs is fairly limited. However, they can usually reach certain spots behind the head and on the flanks. That way they rarely miss a spot when grooming.

NO LIMITS TO CLEANING Hamsters use their teeth to nibble through their fur, so they can keep even sensitive areas like the anus or the external genitalia clean.

in the coat, that may indicate a disease. Only owners of Teddy Bear hamsters have to do a little more.

Coat care: Since the Golden Hamster spends so much time grooming herself, human owners seldom have to intervene in caring for their little friend's coat. If you pay regular attention to your hamster and take note of soiled areas or changes in her coat, there's not much else for you to do. Wet fur, especially around the anus, is a sign of illness (see pages 44 and 46) and merits special attention.

Extra grooming for long-haired hamsters: Teddy Bear hamsters need special attention because their genetically programmed behavior does not adequately provide for grooming their long hair. As a result, they cannot give their beautiful coat the care it requires by themselves. The long hair becomes matted, especially around

the anus, or bits of food get trapped in it. You usually cannot remove the dirt with a comb or brush. Besides, your Teddy Bear will be less than enthusiastic about such activities. That means you have to take action. You'll get the best results as a hamster hairdresser with a small pair of curved scissors. Don't worry about trimming off too much, because it doesn't take long for the hair to grow back. From the time your Teddy Bear is young, get her used to having you trim the hair around her anus. This way you'll prevent infections in that area.

Nail care: The nails of the Golden Hamster should wear down on their own. As a rule, they don't need to be trimmed, which is not the case for animals like guinea pigs.

The hamster has an innate need to scratch, which wears down the nails. It is important that you always put branches as well as toys made of

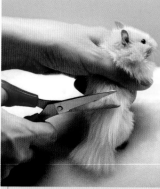

1 IMMOBILIZE **This is the correct way to hold the hamster with one hand, for example when trimming her hair. Don't squeeze her too tightly.**

2 COMB **Long-haired breeds need special coat care! Keep a firm grip on the hamster, who should be used to you by now, and carefully brush out the coat in the direction of growth.**

3 TRIM THE HAIR **It is better to trim off heavily matted hair than to brush it out and hurt the hamster. The hair grows back quickly.**

wood, clay, or aircrete (see pages 52–53) in the cage. The Golden Hamster can wear down her nails on them. If your hamster takes an interest in her sand bath (see Tip, right), this also helps with nail care. Nevertheless, check the length of your pet's nails once a month. If you think they are too long, please don't trim them yourself. The risk of injury and infection is too great. Besides, the animal has to be immobilized to do it, which is very stressful for her. See a veterinarian, who will give you further tips for nail care and will also trim the nails properly.

Dental care: Don't worry—Golden Hamsters don't need to have their teeth brushed. If you include branches and small pieces of wood in the cage, your hamster will be able to wear down her continually growing incisors.

Pros and cons of mineral stones: A perennial topic of discussion among hamster lovers is whether it is necessary or useful to hang up a mineral stone in the cage or add vitamins and minerals to the drinking water. Pet stores sell mineral stones and drinking water supplements. In my opinion, both are unnecessary. A varied diet provides the Golden Hamster with adequate amounts of vitamins and minerals.

Dental abnormalities: Abnormal alignment of teeth is rare in Golden Hamsters. When you get your hamster, make sure that the teeth are aligned properly. Abnormalities cannot be corrected. If you notice misaligned teeth later, the best thing to do is ask your veterinarian. He or she may suggest a solution.

The Hydrophobic Hamster

TIPS FROM
HAMSTER EXPERT
Peter Fritzsche

BATHING HAMSTERS? Please don't get the idea of bathing your Golden Hamster. I strongly advise against it. Although, in principle, it is possible in warm water—like most mammals, Golden Hamsters can swim well—a bath is very stressful for the animal. Hamsters are, by nature, ill equipped for the aquatic life. Their coat dries very slowly, making it likely that they will catch cold. Even the use of a hair dryer or heat lamp is no solution because it is difficult to find the right temperature, and the hamster can easily become overheated.

SAND BATH ALTERNATIVE? Sometimes a sand bath is recommended for Golden Hamsters. It certainly can't hurt, but unlike dwarf hamsters or chinchillas, Golden Hamsters rarely use their sand bath. Test it yourself: Place a shallow dish with chinchilla bath sand (from the pet store) in the cage. If the hamster merely happens upon it by accident, but doesn't use it to take a bath, you can feel free to take it out again.

Cleaning the Hamster's Cage

When you clean the cage, you run the risk of stressing the hamster unnecessarily if you overdo it. She can actually distinguish her individual scent from other odors, and she remembers the exact type and arrangement of the furnishings in her cage. A change brought about by new bedding or a different placement or odor of the objects in the cage upsets her. For example, as we discovered at our Institute, new bedding causes the heart rate of the animals to rise.

Schedule for Cage Maintenance

Compared with other pets, caring for a Golden Hamster's cage is very easy, if you follow a few rules.

Check the food every day: Refill the hamster's empty food bowl with a mixed-seed diet. Take a peek inside the nest box. You can leave any hoarded seeds and grains you find there, but you should remove leftover fresh foods. Check to see that the water bottle is full. During your inspection, don't rearrange anything in the cage.

The Golden Hamster is happy in a spacious cage with several levels and lots of toys to keep her busy. A monthly cleaning is adequate.

Clean the toilet area every three days: The hamster usually establishes a toilet area in her cage. Remove the bedding from this corner and replace it with fresh shavings.

Major food inspection once a week: Remove all food from the bowls and clean them carefully with hot water or in the dishwasher. Empty the water bottle, wash it thoroughly with hot water using a bottle brush but no dish detergent, and refill it with tap water.

Clean the cage once a month: When you do this, your pet must be banished from the cage, for good or ill. If you don't have a travel carrier, another box with walls at least 12 inches (30 cm) high will serve the purpose. In a pinch, you can even let the Golden Hamster wait in a bucket with a bit of old bedding. Put some used bedding from the cage in the "waiting room" and add a cardboard box where the hamster can hide. Remove everything from the cage. Clean wooden objects with a dry brush. Scrub objects made of plastic or clay with hot water and a brush. Remove all the bedding along with hoarded food, but set aside a bit of the old bedding. Clean the bottom tray with hot water and a brush. If the tray is very dirty, you can use a little bit of neutral detergent.

The use of special disinfectants is not necessary. For stubborn dirt, especially in the toilet area, soften up the spots with white vinegar. You can also use diluted vinegar to clean the wire top of the cage. Let everything dry well before putting it away. First add a new layer of substrate and spread some of the old bedding over it. Then put all furnishings back in their original place. Finally, put fresh food in the cage. After you have returned the little occupant to her cage, she'll need a day of rest to get her bearings again. Then she'll rush around marking everything with her personal scent.

A travel carrier makes a comfortable "waiting room" while you are giving the hamster's cage a thorough cleaning.

When the Golden Hamster Gets Sick

Golden Hamsters are not especially susceptible to disease and have a relatively robust immune system. In the wild they sometimes have to cope with extreme climate conditions. If we try to meet their husbandry requirements as closely as possible, then our pets will rarely get sick. On the other hand, treatment of a seriously ill Golden Hamster is fairly difficult. In any case, speed is of the essence. Don't wait too long before visiting the veterinarian. With serious ailments, the veterinarian often has no other choice than to euthanize the hamster to spare her unnecessary suffering. Find out beforehand which veterinarians in your area have experience treating small animals. The natural remedies recommended in many pet care manuals (for instance, Bach Flower Remedies) can, at most, accompany expert veterinary treatment but not replace it!

Be prepared when you go for the appointment. The veterinarian might ask you the following questions:
› How long have you had the animal? Do you know approximately how old she is?
› How large is the hamster cage?
› Has the animal's weight changed?
› What changes (see Checklist opposite) have you noticed in her?
› What do you normally feed your hamster?
› Is the hamster eating normally, very little, or not at all?
› What were you feeding her before the illness?
› Has the hamster had contact with other animals?
› Has the hamster ever been sick before?
› What measures have you already taken?

Diseases of Hamsters

In my experience, the following diseases are the most common among Golden Hamsters:

Mite infestations and fungal infections: Does the hamster seem to be scratching herself a lot and running around restlessly in her cage? A scruffy coat, hair loss in certain spots, or reddened and flaky skin can be caused by an infestation of hair-follicle mites or mange mites. A precise diagnosis can be made only by microscopic examination of the parasites. You can see these tiny arachnids by

A wet bottom usually indicates diarrhea.
Go to the veterinarian right away!

holding the hamster over a sheet of white paper and stroking her coat with your fingers or better yet with a comb.

A mite infestation usually indicates a weakened immune response in the animal, so you should check for poor husbandry (cage too small, dirty food, generally poor nutrition, stress). Excessive cleanliness can also prevent the hamster from building up immunity. Don't try to treat the problem yourself with solutions or sprays; instead, go to the veterinarian. With fungal infections, wash and disinfect your hands immediately after touching the animal or working in the cage.

Diarrhea: If the hamster's feces are soft or even watery and the anal region is soiled, this indicates diarrhea. The hamster is less active than before and also eats less. A bacterial infection, caused for instance by *Salmonella*, is usually present. Poisoning as a result of ingesting toxic houseplants can also lead to diarrhea. Have you recently switched foods or fed a lot of fresh food? Did the hamster eat anything from the ground during out-of-cage time? The first thing you can do is eliminate all fresh food and clean the hamster's bottom to prevent infection. You must go to the veterinarian within the next 24 hours.

Colds: The hamster sneezes, her nose runs, and you hear a whistling sound when she breathes. Here, too, the cause is usually improper husbandry. Was the animal exposed to a draft or extreme variations in temperature? You can speed up the recovery process by shining a heat lamp on one part of the cage. Keep it far enough away from the cage that the temperature doesn't climb above 86°F (30°C), even directly beneath the lamp. The hamster must be able to move away from the heat. The veterinarian may also prescribe antibiotics for her.

Signs of **Serious Illness**

GO TO THE VETERINARIAN!

BEHAVIOR	apathetic, sits in the corner, no longer active even at night; especially aggressive and more irritable than usual; eats little or nothing; trembles or is unusually jumpy; abnormal gait; scratches constantly
APPEARANCE	wet bottom; swollen, hard, tight abdomen; weight loss of more than 0.25 ounce (7 g) in one week or clear signs of emaciation; diarrhea; swellings on the body; unnaturally hunched posture; overgrown nails
COAT AND SKIN	ruffled, unkempt coat; excessive hair loss; flaky skin
EYES	eyes are dry, reddened, watering, or protruding; eyelids are stuck together or half closed
NOSE	nasal discharge; unusual breathing noises or sneezing
MOUTH	drooling; crusty lips; cheek pouches cannot be completely emptied; overgrown or misaligned teeth

Wet tail: This intestinal ailment, more common in young Golden Hamsters, is characterized by wet fur around the tail and diarrhea. One possible trigger is infection by fecal coliform bacteria. The disease can develop when the animal is under too much stress. The treatment is the same as for diarrhea: Eliminate fresh foods from the diet and go to the veterinarian immediately!

Impacted cheek pouches: If your Golden Hamster keeps trying unsuccessfully to empty her cheek pouches, and refuses food, her cheek pouches might be impacted. She may have eaten something sticky, like gummy candies. If this is not treated, it can lead to inflammation and possibly abscesses of the cheek pouches.

Tumors: If you feel a hard spot or a lump when running your hands over the hamster, it might be a tumor. These occur spontaneously, especially in older animals. Ask your veterinarian if the tumor

can or must be removed surgically. If the hamster is more than 18 months old and the tumor is already fairly large, it is usually better to put the animal out of her misery.

Cheilitis: The corners of the mouth, the lips, and the nose of the hamster are reddened or crusty. Because of an improper or unbalanced diet, tiny cracks have formed in the skin and then become colonized by bacteria or fungi. The veterinarian will prescribe an ointment for your hamster.

Broken bones: The veterinarian needs an X-ray to determine the extent of the injury. Unfortunately, fractures of the limbs or injuries of the spine are rarely treatable; it is usually better to euthanize the animal. Only minor fractures (like those of the toes) can heal completely.

Heatstroke: If the hamster is exposed to high temperatures or direct sun for an extended period, she suffers metabolic collapse. She lies on the floor apathetically and her breathing is rapid. Quickly move the animal to a cooler place and moisten her muzzle with water.

Eye ailments: If the hamster's eyes are watering excessively, protruding, or inflamed, this can indicate a bacterial or viral infection. The infection is often from a minor injury to the eye, caused by something like improper bedding or hard stalks of hay. Only your veterinarian can help here. He or she will probably prescribe treatment with eye ointment and explain to you how to use it. Surgery may be necessary in severe cases. Prevent problems like this by using suitable bedding.

Bite wounds: If, contrary to recommendations, you do not keep each Golden Hamster in a separate cage, or if you are attempting to breed a female who is not ready to mate, this can lead to

A heat lamp can often promote the healing process. Be sure to monitor the temperature regularly to prevent overheating!

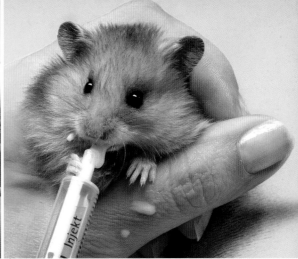

A powder from the veterinarian helps to treat mite infestations. Be careful not to get any in the hamster's eyes, mouth, or nose.

You can give your Golden Hamster medications or nutritional supplements for her intestinal flora relatively easily with a plastic syringe (minus the needle, naturally).

bite wounds, usually in the anal or genital area and on the flanks. Separate the animals immediately. Smaller injuries heal by themselves. You should have the veterinarian examine larger, bleeding wounds.

Diabetes: This disease can also affect hamsters. It is definitely caused by an improper diet too high in sugar or fat. The disease is not easy to recognize. If your hamster is already fairly old, overweight, or has a high urine output, this can indicate diabetes. The veterinarian will make the final diagnosis.

Nursing care: Above all, a sick hamster needs rest and constant warmth. If using a heat lamp, it should always shine on just one part of the cage. Use a cotton swab or dampened absorbent paper to remove dirt from the head or anal area. You can give a liquid or powdered medication by sprinkling it on a mealworm. Be sure to ask your veterinarian for advice. Unfortunately, animals often die because of incorrect treatment.

Caution: **Danger of Infection**

DISEASES TRANSMITTED BY ANIMALS
Fortunately, there is not much danger of Golden Hamsters catching diseases from other animals. Aside from harmless fungal infections, the only disease reported is a very rare infection of the central nervous system, lymphocytic chorio-meningitis (LCM). This usually affects young hamsters that have had contact with infected mice, for instance in animal breeding facilities. Although in recent years there have been only isolated cases of infection in people who had occupational exposure to rodents, pregnant women should avoid contact with hamsters as a precaution.

Abnormal Behavior in Golden Hamsters

If Golden Hamsters are not kept properly, or if their cage environment does not provide enough stimulation, they have a tendency to develop behavioral problems. You can do a lot to keep your hamster happy and healthy.

Stereotypic Behavior

When an animal performs the same actions again and again over a prolonged period with no obvious purpose, we call this "stereotypy." This type of behavior is a reaction to a stimulus-poor environment. For example, some Golden Hamsters chew incessantly on the cage wires, and nothing can get them to stop. Others run back and forth over the same path, usually along one side of the cage. Still others keep trying to scale a corner of their glass terrarium or aquarium. Stereotypic behaviors like these are caused by inadequate, usually monotonous living conditions. By providing the hamster with an enriched environment and plenty of activities (see pages 50–59), you can effectively prevent behavioral problems like these. Once the Golden Hamster makes a habit of an abnormal behavior, it is very difficult or impossible to get her to stop. A new, larger cage, more activities, and out-of-cage time are options for redirecting the Golden Hamster's attention. Wire chewing, for example, is dramatically reduced by putting an exercise wheel in the cage.

The Golden Hamster is very shy: If your Golden Hamster is still young, there is no need to worry. Just give her a bit more time to settle in, and never try to force her to do anything. You can win her trust only by approaching her calmly and carefully. If, however, this behavior appears rather suddenly in a pet that had been behaving normally, it could be caused by an illness. Check the hamster's appearance and body weight. You might have to consult your veterinarian. If there are no signs of illness, the only remaining possibility is that some external situation caused the animal stress. Have you or somebody else disturbed her repeatedly when she was sleeping during the day? Is it possible that she is no longer being handled as gently as necessary? Young children, in particular, are often impatient and expect too much of their new companion. Have a talk with your children about this and explain to them that the hamster needs to get used to her caregivers and must never be awakened when she is asleep.

My Golden Hamster bites: Although Golden Hamsters rarely bite, it is possible that you or your child will be bitten by the hamster. These injuries heal quickly, and special treatment is usually unnecessary. The animals sometimes bite when they are handled clumsily or disturbed when sleeping. Then, too, if a finger is poked through the cage wires, they are eager to test the new "food" with their teeth. If the Golden Hamster becomes unfriendly, and keeps trying to bite, it is probably because, as already described, too little patience was exercised when she was settling in.

CAREFUL, NIPPY "My Golden Hamster still isn't tame, and when I want to handle her, she bites. What should I do?" Young hamster lovers, in particular, have this problem. Unfortunately, there is no ready remedy. Young Golden Hamsters are sometimes very skittish and have trouble becoming acclimated. The only thing that helps is to be patient and approach them with care. Never pick up the hamster right away. Make sure, especially, that she can sleep undisturbed during the day.

ABNORMAL Golden Hamsters that are kept in glass or plastic containers (like aquariums) sometimes display unusual behavior. They run back and forth along the walls and try to scale them. The hamster can sometimes be persuaded to give up stereotypic behaviors like this with the right equipment, such as an exercise wheel. It is a good idea to move the animal to a wire cage; the ventilation is better, anyway.

SHY HAMSTER Whereas some Golden Hamsters are especially aggressive, others prefer to hide. For these shy types, it's important that you try to win and keep their trust with lots of patience.

Always on the Move

In the wild, Golden Hamsters are constantly faced with new challenges. That's why it is so important to provide plenty of opportunity for appropriate activity when keeping a hamster as a pet. It's good for your little friend, and you'll have lots of fun watching his antics.

The Fit Golden Hamster

Foraging for food, searching for a mate, and evading enemies are the most important tasks facing Golden Hamsters in the wild. Depending on where their burrow is located, they overcome a wide variety of obstacles in the process.

Scientific Findings

Only recently have we zoologists begun to study the natural behavior of Golden Hamsters living in the wild. Modern technology has helped us with this research. On one of our expeditions, we outfitted Golden Hamsters with miniature radio transmitters. These sent out regular signals that we were able to receive with an antenna and radio equipment. This way the Golden Hamsters revealed their whereabouts to us. Using another method, we implanted tiny chips no bigger than a grain of rice in some Golden Hamsters, which enabled us to record the little rodents whenever they exited or entered their burrow. They had to pass antennas and photoelectric sensors that we had installed or were observed with minicameras. We discovered that Golden Hamsters love to be on the move. Males searching for females, in particular, cover fairly large distances at night.

Hamsters in Captivity

Thanks to scientific research, we now know that Golden Hamsters need plenty of exercise and variety to live a healthy and normal life in captivity. A sufficiently large cage and a richly structured environment as well as frequent, supervised out-of-cage time add the necessary spice to the hamster's life and help avoid stereotypic behavior (see page 48).

Hamster, Stay Active!

Challenge your hamster by giving him a cage with a variety of toys to keep him busy. Pet stores carry a wide assortment of accessories for the Golden Hamster's cage.

What Golden Hamsters Like

Golden Hamsters need plenty of stimulation when they live in a cage; otherwise they develop behavioral problems and are more likely to get sick because they get too little exercise and have too little to do.

Do hamsters play? Sometimes people refer to hamster cage accessories as "toys." Golden Hamsters don't play, though; instead, they explore their environment for things to eat or raw materials for building a nest. With the right cage accessories,

Aircrete is a sturdy material, yet it's easy to work with. Your Golden Hamster will be certain to love aircrete bridges, tunnels, and towers.

you can encourage this exploratory behavior and thus ensure that your hamster stays active and enjoys new experiences.

Appropriate accessories: In principle, any object or material that cannot injure or endanger the hamster is suitable. Favorites include things made of untreated wood, potting clay, sisal, or nontoxic modeling clay. Unprinted cardboard is also appropriate for the hamster cage. Multilevel cages with small ladders or seesaws satisfy the hamsters' need to climb; after all, in the wild they can clamber out of their burrow with lightning speed. Hamsters have an insatiable urge to crawl into everything or at least poke their head into holes or other openings. That's why they love tree trunks, sturdy branches, or small boxes with openings. The openings should be no smaller than 1.75 inches (4.5 cm) in diameter so that the animals can't get stuck. Avoid crevices, too. Make sure the accessories have no protruding nails, screws, or sharp ends that could hurt the animals. Being rodents, Golden Hamsters will usually try to gnaw anything in their cage to bits, so they shouldn't be able to expose nails or other hazards by their chewing. It's better to buy or make accessories that are held together with glue.

Favorite sports: running and digging: Tunnel systems in the cage are a favorite with all Golden Hamsters (see page 18). After all, in the wild the individual chambers of the Golden Hamster's burrow are connected by tunnels.

That's why tunnels are well suited to their natural behavior. Golden Hamsters also seem to like having contact with the tunnel walls; it probably gives them a feeling of security. In fact, they use the tunnels for sleeping when they are tired of all that running. Make sure that you provide cardboard or plastic tunnels for your hamster. In addition, you can build a little play area in the cage, using different types and arrangements of flooring materials. Your hamster will love running across it and digging in it. For example, you could use bark mulch, pebbles of various sizes, sand, cork, and a carpet of twigs. You can also offer the hamster this assortment of materials in small dishes at various spots in the cage. He'll have a great time digging in them.

Build it yourself with wood: The material of choice for cage accessories is wood. Pet stores offer a wide selection of assorted types for the hamster cage. If you have the time and inclination, homemade toys are no problem, either. You could start by building a nest box. Accessories like wooden seesaws, bridges, and crawl-through blocks are also easy to make. It's best to paint the pieces with special nontoxic paint for children's toys. Then they will last longer and be easier to clean. You can also use branches from fruit trees for your creations. Cut pieces about 4 inches (10 cm) long from branches about half an inch (1 cm) in diameter. Drill through the branches at either end and string several of these pieces on two wires. Now you can hang them up in the cage as hammocks or use them as bridges.

Creative Hamster Accesssories

TIPS FROM
HAMSTER EXPERT
Peter Fritzsche

DO YOU ENJOY WORKING WITH CLAY? Craft and hobby shops sell high-quality clay in shades of white and brown. With a little practice, you can use it to make food bowls, huts, bridges, or more complicated structures. Let your imagination run wild. Make sure that the openings for the hamster to crawl through are at least 1.75 inches (4.5 cm) in diameter. Keep in mind that clay shrinks when it is fired. Depending on the material, your creations can be baked in the kitchen oven at about 480°F (250°C) or air dried.

BUILDING WITH AIRCRETE This easily worked material, also known as autoclaved aerated concrete, is sold under a variety of brand names, including Aercon and Xella in North America and Ytong in Europe. Aircrete can be worked like wood and is safe for Golden Hamsters. With a saw, hammer, chisel, and a little effort, you can easily make interesting objects for your hamster. You'll enjoy seeing your pet's reaction to these new homemade toys and watching him use them.

Fun and Games for Hamsters

Nothing is worse for your Golden Hamster than boredom. To keep it at bay, start out right by offering your pet a variety of toys and exercise equipment.

1 Tunnels

Golden Hamsters love to crawl through tunnels. Openings in the sides make it more fun to go exploring while improving ventilation. These tunnels don't have to be made of wood. Cardboard tubes, like those from paper towel rolls, are also popular. Your Golden Hamster can just chew them into shape however he likes.

2 Obstacles

In the wild, hamsters have to overcome many obstacles to reach their food. If your hamster is used to you, feel free to let him "work" for a treat and tempt him over barriers like these.

3 Exercise Wheel

A hamster on an exercise wheel has almost become iconic. Not surprisingly, there has been a great deal of discussion about the advantages and disadvantages of an exercise wheel in the hamster cage. One scientific study compared Golden Hamsters with and without exercise wheels. In addition to reducing stereotypic behaviors as discussed earlier (see page 48), the wheel was found to increase the Golden Hamsters' well-being. They were slimmer and reproduced more successfully. That's why I definitely recommend that you install an exercise wheel in the cage. It should be about 12 inches (30 cm) in diameter, and the running surface should be at least 3 inches (8 cm) wide. Metal exercise wheels are bad because they force the animals to run on wire rungs; they can slip off and hurt themselves. Make sure that the running surface is solid and that one side of the exercise wheel is completely closed.

4 Digging Box

Digging is one of the Golden Hamster's favorite and most important behaviors. It's hard to do in the soft bedding of the cage, though. That's why your hamster will love his sandbox. Here he can dig passageways and search for hidden food. Moisten the sand to prevent it from caving in right away.

5 Wooden Towers

Golden Hamsters normally don't climb trees. All the same, animals living in the wild can scamper up vertical tunnels in their burrow very quickly. Pet hamsters can do this at home, too.

Unsuitable "Toys"

WATCH OUT Check all objects to make sure they pose no risk of injury, are made of nontoxic materials, and allow adequate circulation of air. "Hamster balls," "exercise balls," and "hamster cars," which unfortunately are still available, are totally inappropriate because they confine the animal in a small compartment from which he can't escape. That is cruel to the animal!

Hamster Playground

Hay Basket

Put your pet's hay in a small basket. The feeding area also doubles as a hamster hideout.

Digging Box

Fill a box with damp sand for digging and scratching. Hide a few little treats in it, too.

Walls

The walls are formed by boards at least 12 inches (30 cm) high that slide into grooves in the corner posts. This makes it easy to set up and take down.

Floor

Carpet or fabric remnants (like old sheets) make ideal floor coverings.

Treasure Chest

Use your imagination when designing this box. There's plenty for the Golden Hamst to investigate, and every compartment holds a new surprise.

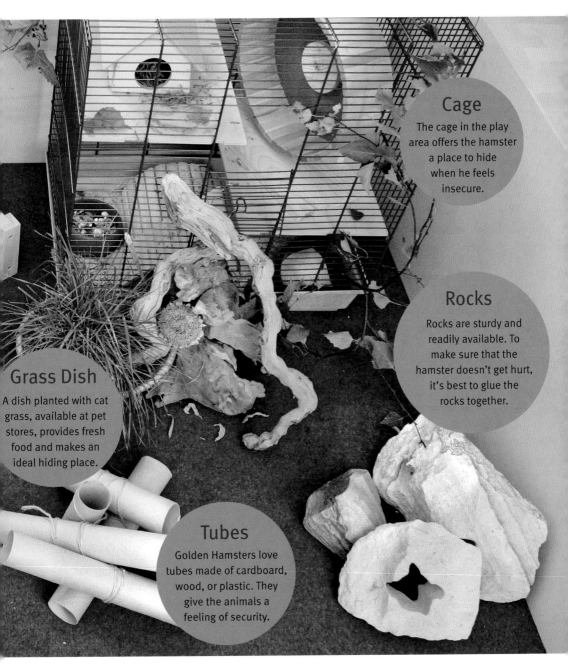

Cage

The cage in the play area offers the hamster a place to hide when he feels insecure.

Rocks

Rocks are sturdy and readily available. To make sure that the hamster doesn't get hurt, it's best to glue the rocks together.

Grass Dish

A dish planted with cat grass, available at pet stores, provides fresh food and makes an ideal hiding place.

Tubes

Golden Hamsters love tubes made of cardboard, wood, or plastic. They give the animals a feeling of security.

Free Roaming Time Indoors

In addition to stocking your Golden Hamster's cage with toys and activities, allowing your pet some free-roaming time indoors provides a lovely change of pace. Never let him run free in the yard, out in a meadow, or even on the balcony, though! These places are too dangerous for the little rodent. Golden Hamsters are burrowing animals, so it is an easy matter for them to dig their way out of their enclosure, if they haven't already discovered a hole or hiding place through which they can disappear, never to be seen again. It's also easy for them to become infected with parasites outdoors and get sick.

Freedom for the Cage Dweller

Most Golden Hamsters love to breathe in the scents of the great wide world and explore new things when they're outside the cage. Give your pet this opportunity, either in a hamster-proofed room or in a special play area.

Out-of-cage time indoors: Even indoors there are any number of dangers lying in wait for your Golden Hamster, but you can do something about them. Check the following: electrical outlets, power strips or electrical wires lying on the floor, sharp or pointed objects, burning candles, and anything that could fall on the animal. The hamster should not be able to eat any plants or cut flowers, because many of them are poisonous for him. Curtains or drapes should be out of reach. Close off any open crevices, gaps, or openings—before the hamster can disappear into them—with a strip of cardboard at least 12 inches (30 cm) high. Put away vases that the animal could climb into but then not be able to get out of again. In the winter, watch out for heaters that are switched on. Toxic substances that the hamster could nibble on should be inaccessible. If dogs or cats live in your home, they should not be allowed near the hamster. Carpet is ideal for the play area; parquet flooring, laminate flooring, or other smooth surfaces are not suitable. To protect your carpet, cover it with an old sheet that you can simply launder later.

The play area: The nicest option, and certainly the easiest on your nerves, is to construct a playground (see pages 56–57) by getting yourself some fairly long boards 12 inches (30 cm) high and using them to lay out the play area. Make sure the boards can't fall over!

Adventure beyond the cage! And in case you haven't heard, books aren't just for reading.

How do I design a play area? Give your imagination free rein. Here are some suggestions to inspire you:

› Build a "hamster castle" in the middle of the room. You could use a shallow box with some bedding and an entrance (a ladder or a cut-out doorway). Place accessories like branches, rocks, or a hamster hut inside.

› Fasten together an assortment of pieces of wood or a stack of tubes with adhesive tape.

› Make a maze using rocks or pieces of wood. In the middle of the maze, put the hamster's favorite snack as a reward.

› Plant a shallow dish with grass seeds or cereal grains. As soon as the plants are 2 to 4 inches (5–10 cm) tall, give it to your hamster as a meadow to play in.

› Hang pieces of carrot or cucumber on a variety of branches or roots so that the hamster can climb up to get them.

› Build a cave system by cutting holes in boxes and connecting them with cardboard tubes (the tubes from paper towel or toilet paper rolls work well).

› Set up a dish with sand or a mixture of wood shavings and garden peat where the hamster can dig and burrow. Hide tasty tidbits in it.

Supervised out-of-cage time: The first time you let your hamster out of the cage to play, place the cage on the floor and open the door to the wide world of the room or the play area. That's better than removing the hamster from the cage. Keep an eye on him from a reasonable distance. You may have overlooked a hazard, or the hamster might get himself into a tight spot and you will have to intervene. Then the hamster will begin to investigate the room or the play area and enjoy his freedom.

As everybody knows, you can catch mice with cheese. And you can set out treats in the room to lure an escaped hamster.

Help! – **My Golden Hamster Is Gone!**

THE HAMSTER ESCAPED—NOW WHAT?
Despite every precaution, most hamster owners are familiar with their pets' unintended out-of-cage time. Above all, stay calm and don't run around the house in a panic. The first thing to do is close all doors to the rooms in question. Listen for noises and investigate them. To capture the animal, use a plastic container, cardboard box, or something similarly cave-like. Place it near the animal. Then close in from the other side with your hand or another object to make the animal run for the shelter of the "cave." You will find additional advice on the inside back cover.

Organizations

> American Society for the Prevention of Cruelty to Animals (ASPCA)
> *www.aspca.org*

> California Hamster Association
> *www.geocities.com/CalHamAssoc*

> The Humane Society of the United States (HSUS)
> *www.hsus.org*

> National Hamster Council
> *www.hamsters-uk.org*

> Pet Web Site
> *www.petwebsite.com/hamsters.asp*

Books

> Bartlett, Patricia. *The Hamster Handbook* (Barron's Pet Handbooks). Hauppauge, NY: Barron's Educational Series, 2003.

> Fritzsche, Peter. *My Hamster* (My Pet). Hauppauge, NY: Barron's Educational Series, 2008.

> Hollimann, Peter. *My Hamster and Me* (For the Love of Animals). Hauppauge, NY: Barron's Educational Series, 2001.

> Kahn, Cynthia M., ed. *The Merck/Merial Manual for Pet Health*, Home Edition. Whitehouse Station, NJ: Merck & Co., 2007.

> Siegel, Harold I., ed. *The Hamster: Reproduction and Behavior*. New York: Plenum Press, 1985.

Magazines

> *Hamsters* (Popular Critters Series). Irvine, CA: BowTie Magazines.

Important **Information**

> Sick Golden Hamster If you see signs of illness in your hamster, take him to the veterinarian.

> Danger of Infection Only a few diseases can be transmitted to humans. Let your physician know about your contact with animals. This is especially true if you are bitten by an animal.

> Animal Hair Allergies Some people are allergic to animal hair. If you are not certain, ask your physician before buying a hamster.

German edition by: Peter Fritzsche
Photography by: Regina Kuhn
Published originally under the title *Goldhamster* in the series *GU Tierratgerer*
© 2007 by Gräfe and Unzer Verlag GmbH, Munich, Germany

English translation © Copyright 2009 by Barron's Educational Series, Inc.
English translation by Mary D. Lynch

All inquiries should be addressed to:
Barron's Educational Series, Inc.
250 Wireless Boulevard
Hauppauge, NY 11788
www.barronseduc.com

ISBN-13: 978-0-7641-4285-7
ISBN-10: 0-7641-4285-2

Library of Congress Control No.: 2009011233

PRINTED IN CHINA
9 8 7 6 5 4 3 2 1

The Author

Dr. Peter Fritzsche received his doctorate in biology and is a member of the scientific staff at the Institute of Zoology, Martin Luther University of Halle-Wittenberg, Germany. He has been doing research on the behavioral biology of hamsters for about 30 years and is an internationally recognized hamster expert. In private life, he enthusiastically shares his home with an assortment of pets, above all, naturally, hamsters.

The Photographer

Regina Kuhn is a freelance photo-designer and works as an animal photographer for major publishers and magazines. All photos in this book are Ms. Kuhn's with the exception of Peter Fritzsche, pages 6, 7, 8; and Oliver Giel, pages 15, 16.

Acknowledgments

The author is grateful to the late Professor Rolf Gatterman for the opportunity to pursue scientific research on the Golden Hamster.

The photographer and publisher wish to thank the Zoo & Angler Center, Eisennach; Sally Matern, Hochdorf; and Jenny Garbrecht, Göringen, all in Germany.

SOS – What Should I Do?

The Golden Hamster Bites

IMMEDIATELY Did you disturb her while she was sleeping? This is stressful for her, and she will defend herself. **LONG TERM** She might not be quite used to people yet, or something may be bothering her. Be patient and continue to treat her with care.

The Hamster Is Sick

IMMEDIATELY If the hamster is noticeably withdrawn, he is probably seriously ill. Watch him closely. If he has diarrhea, immediately stop giving him fresh foods, refill the water bottle, and take him to the veterinarian. For colds, avoid drafts and increase the room temperature slightly. See the veterinarian!

Unexpected Offspring

IMMEDIATELY You probably acquired a pregnant female. Try not to disturb the mother and her babies. Stay as far away from the cage as possible. The hamster mother needs lots of protein in her diet now. Unfortunately, an inexperienced mother sometimes eats her litter.

The Golden Hamster Has Escaped

IMMEDIATELY If you know where he is, try to tempt him with his favorite food. You can also place a dark container, such as a cardboard tube, near his hiding place and wait a bit. If you don't know where he's hiding, scatter treats in the center of all likely rooms and check them regularly. Another trick: Place a towel over the top of a bucket and put his favorite food on it. Lean a board against the bucket to act as a ramp, then leave the room. Ideally, the hamster won't be able to resist; he'll climb up to the edge of the bucket and fall in, and the towel will act as a cushion.

The Hamster Chews on the Cage Wires

LONG TERM This behavior is usually caused by a cage that is too small or by too little opportunity for activity. Liven things up in the cage a bit with an exercise wheel and a good tunnel system. It is difficult, though, to cure this behavioral problem in Golden Hamsters.

JOHNSON
&
PFLUG

No 2 copies